We hope this book has been informative and helpful on your journey to understanding and celebrating older adults. Thank you for your interest and support!

Title: The Roots of the Game-Tracing the Evolution of Football's Leading Scorers
Subtitle: The Mavericks and Visionaries Who Shaped the Beautiful Game

Series: Striking Gold: Top Scorers in Football before the 1980s
By Michael Jaynes

"Football is a simple game. Twenty-two men chase a ball for 90 minutes and at the end, the Germans always win."
Gary Lineker

"Some people think football is a matter of life and death. I assure you, it's much more serious than that."
Bill Shankly

"Football was different back then. It was more about the love of the game and the joy of scoring goals than it was about money and fame."
Pele

"The early days of football were a magical time. There was a purity to the sport that has been lost in modern times."
Bobby Charlton

"The great goal scorers of the past were true artists. They had a sense of poetry and beauty that is rarely seen in the game today."
Eusebio

"The goal scorers of the past were not just great athletes, they were also great storytellers. They could create drama and tension with every shot they took."
Nándor Hidegkuti

"The ball is round, the game lasts 90 minutes, and everything else is just theory."
Josef Herberger

Table of Contents

Introduction

Overview of the book and its purpose

Football, also known as soccer in some parts of the world, is one of the most popular sports globally, with millions of fans and players worldwide. The sport has a rich history that dates back over a century, and during this time, numerous players have made their mark on the game. In this book, we take an in-depth look at the early years of some of the greatest goal scorers in football history and explore their rise to fame.

Overview of the book and its purpose:

The purpose of this book is to provide a unique and in-depth look into the early years of some of the greatest goal scorers in football history. From the humble beginnings of their careers to their rise to fame, readers will gain a deeper understanding of what it takes to become a prolific goal scorer.

The book will be divided into six chapters, each dedicated to a different player. We will start with Pele, who is widely regarded as one of the greatest football players of all time. From there, we will move on to other notable players such as Dixie Dean, Luigi Riva, Bobby Charlton, Evaristo de Macedo, and Nándor Hidegkuti. By exploring the lives and careers of these players, we hope to provide readers with a comprehensive understanding of the roots of their success.

Throughout the book, we will examine each player's early life, including their introduction to football, as well as their career highlights, personal struggles, and notable achievements. We will also delve into each player's playing style and strengths, and how they impacted the sport.

Additionally, we will discuss the legacy and influence each player had on the sport, both in their respective countries and on a global scale. By doing so, we hope to give readers a broader understanding of the impact that these players had on football and how their legacy continues to shape the sport today.

Whether you are a die-hard fan of the game or simply enjoy reading about inspiring journeys, the "Roots of" series is sure to captivate and inspire. Through this book, we hope to offer a unique perspective on some of the greatest goal scorers in football history and provide readers with a deeper understanding of the roots of their success.

Brief history of football/soccer and its evolution

Before we dive into the early years of some of the greatest goal scorers in football history, it's essential to understand the sport's history and evolution. Football, also known as soccer in some parts of the world, has a rich and fascinating history that spans over a century. In this chapter, we will provide a brief history of football and its evolution, from its origins to the present day.

Origins:

The origins of football can be traced back to ancient civilizations, where people played games that involved kicking a ball. However, the modern version of football that we know today originated in England in the mid-19th century. The first documented game of football took place in 1863 when the Football Association was formed.

Evolution:

Over the years, football has undergone several changes and transformations, both in terms of rules and gameplay. In the early years, football was a physical and often violent game, with little regard for players' safety. However, as the game grew in popularity, rules were introduced to make it safer and more enjoyable for players.

One of the most significant changes in football's evolution was the introduction of international competitions.

In 1900, football was included in the Olympic Games for the first time, and in 1930, the first-ever World Cup was held in Uruguay. These competitions helped to raise the profile of the sport and make it a truly global phenomenon.

Another significant change in football's evolution was the introduction of professional leagues. In the early years, football was played by amateur teams, but as the sport grew in popularity, professional leagues were established. The English Football League was formed in 1888, and since then, numerous professional leagues have been established around the world.

In recent years, technology has played a significant role in football's evolution. The introduction of goal-line technology and video assistant referees (VAR) has helped to make the game fairer and more transparent. Additionally, advancements in sports science and technology have enabled players to perform at higher levels and reduce the risk of injury.

Conclusion:

In conclusion, football has a rich and fascinating history that spans over a century. The sport has undergone several changes and transformations, from its origins in ancient civilizations to the present day. As the sport continues to evolve, it's essential to remember and appreciate its history and the impact that it has had on people's lives worldwide.

Importance of scoring goals in football

Scoring goals is the ultimate aim of any football team. Without scoring goals, a team cannot hope to win a match, let alone a competition. In this section, we will explore the importance of scoring goals in football, and how it has evolved over time.

The importance of scoring goals in football cannot be overstated. It is the ultimate objective of the game, and everything else is secondary. A goal changes the course of a game, and often has a psychological impact on both teams. Scoring early in a match can give a team a huge advantage, both in terms of morale and tactics. It forces the opposition to attack more, which can lead to more gaps in their defence, and ultimately more goals for the attacking team.

In the early days of football, the importance of scoring goals was just as significant as it is today. However, the tactics and strategies used to score goals were different. The game was much more physical, and often relied on brute force rather than finesse. Teams would often use long balls to bypass the opposition's defence and create goal-scoring opportunities. This was especially prevalent in English football, where the game was more direct and less technical.

Over time, the importance of scoring goals has remained constant, but the strategies used to achieve this objective have evolved. The game has become more technical, and teams now focus on creating intricate passing moves to break down opposition defences. This has led to a greater emphasis on possession and control, rather than just sheer physicality.

The evolution of football tactics has also led to a greater importance being placed on individual players, especially strikers. Teams now build their attacks around a focal point, a player who can create and score goals. This has led to the development of specialist strikers, who are valued for their ability to finish chances and create opportunities for their teammates.

The importance of scoring goals has also extended beyond just the 90 minutes on the pitch. In modern football, players are often judged on their goal-scoring records, and this can have a huge impact on their careers. Strikers who score consistently are often seen as the most valuable players, and are in high demand from clubs all over the world. This has led to huge transfer fees being paid for the best goal-scorers, and has created a market for specialist goal-scorers.

In conclusion, the importance of scoring goals in football cannot be overstated. It is the ultimate objective of the game, and everything else is secondary. The tactics and strategies used to score goals have evolved over time, but the fundamental importance of putting the ball in the back of the net remains the same. The role of the striker has become more important, and specialist goal-scorers are now highly valued in the modern game.

Chapter 1: Pele - Brazil - 767 goals (656 club + 111 national) - retired 1977

Early life and rise to fame

Edson Arantes do Nascimento, popularly known as Pelé, is widely regarded as one of the greatest football players of all time. Pelé was born in Três Corações, Brazil, on October 23, 1940. From a young age, he showed a natural talent for football, and he started playing for local clubs at the age of 15.

Pelé's rise to fame began when he was spotted by the Brazilian football coach, Waldemar de Brito, who was impressed by his skills and invited him to join Santos, one of the top teams in Brazil, in 1956. At the time, Santos was struggling, but Pelé's arrival changed everything. He made his debut for the club on September 7, 1956, at the age of 15, and scored his first goal in the same game.

Pelé's early performances for Santos were impressive, and he quickly became the team's star player. His first full season with the club, in 1957, was a breakthrough year for both him and Santos. Pelé scored 36 goals in 29 games, and Santos won the Campeonato Paulista, the top state league in São Paulo. The following year, Pelé helped Santos win the Copa Libertadores, the most prestigious club competition in South America, for the first time in the club's history.

Pelé's success on the field brought him widespread fame and recognition in Brazil and around the world. He became known for his dazzling skills, including his speed, agility, and ball control, as well as his powerful and accurate shots. He also had a remarkable ability to read the game and anticipate his opponents' moves, which made him a formidable opponent.

In addition to his skills on the field, Pelé was also admired for his humility and sportsmanship. He was known for his positive attitude, his respect for his opponents, and his commitment to fair play. Off the field, he was a popular figure in Brazil and beyond, and he used his fame to promote charitable causes and social issues.

Overall, Pelé's early life and rise to fame were characterized by his exceptional talent, his dedication to the game, and his positive attitude and sportsmanship. These qualities would continue to define his career in the years to come, as he cemented his place as one of the greatest football players of all time.

Key achievements, including World Cup wins and records

Pele is widely regarded as one of the greatest football players of all time, and his achievements on the field are a testament to his talent and dedication to the sport. In this section, we will take a closer look at some of his key achievements, including his World Cup wins and records.

Pele's first World Cup victory came in 1958, when he was just 17 years old. He played a crucial role in Brazil's success, scoring six goals in the tournament, including two in the final against Sweden. Pele's performance in the World Cup was a revelation, and he quickly became a global superstar.

Four years later, in 1962, Pele led Brazil to their second consecutive World Cup victory. Although he missed most of the tournament due to injury, his presence on the field in the final against Czechoslovakia was enough to inspire his teammates to victory.

Pele's third and final World Cup victory came in 1970, when he was at the peak of his career. He played a pivotal role in Brazil's success, scoring four goals in the tournament, including one in the final against Italy. Pele's performance in the 1970 World Cup is widely regarded as one of the greatest individual performances in the history of the tournament.

In addition to his three World Cup wins, Pele also holds a number of records in the sport. He is the all-time leading scorer for Brazil, with 77 goals in 92 appearances. He is also the only player to have won the World Cup three times as a player, and he is the youngest player to have scored in a World Cup final.

Pele's records don't stop there. He is the only player to have scored more than 1,000 goals in his career, a feat that is unlikely to be matched. He is also the only player to have won the Ballon d'Or three times, an award given to the best player in the world.

Pele's achievements on the field have earned him a place in football history, and his impact on the sport is still felt today. He has inspired generations of players, and his legacy as a football icon continues to grow.

Playing style and impact on the sport

Pele's playing style was unique and impactful, influencing not only Brazilian football but also the game globally. His ability to score goals in a variety of ways and his technical skills on the ball made him a formidable opponent and a joy to watch.

One of the hallmarks of Pele's playing style was his agility and quick footwork. He had the ability to change direction on a dime and could accelerate and decelerate rapidly. This allowed him to outmaneuver defenders and create space for himself and his teammates. His close control of the ball was also exceptional, and he was known for his dribbling skills.

Pele was a versatile player who could play anywhere in the attacking third of the field. He was equally comfortable as a winger, a center forward, or an attacking midfielder. This allowed his coaches to deploy him in a variety of ways, depending on the opposition and the tactical situation. He was also adept at combining with his teammates and could play intricate one-two passes that opened up space and created scoring opportunities.

Another key aspect of Pele's playing style was his finishing ability. He had a powerful shot with both feet and was able to score from a variety of angles and distances. He was also excellent in the air, despite being only 5'8" tall, and scored many goals with his head.

Pele's impact on the sport of football cannot be overstated. His success with the Brazilian national team, including three World Cup victories, helped to elevate the status of the sport in Brazil and around the world. He was a role model for young players and inspired generations of footballers to emulate his style and success.

In addition to his on-field success, Pele was also an ambassador for the sport and worked to promote it around the world. He was a vocal advocate for fair play and sportsmanship, and his positive attitude and charisma helped to make him one of the most beloved figures in the history of the sport.

Overall, Pele's playing style and impact on the sport of football were truly exceptional. His agility, technical skills, and finishing ability made him a dominant force on the field, while his success with the Brazilian national team helped to raise the profile of the sport and inspire generations of players.

Legacy and influence on future players

Pele's legacy and influence on future players can hardly be overstated. Throughout his career, he inspired a generation of young footballers with his skill, athleticism, and sportsmanship, and continues to do so to this day. In this section, we will explore Pele's impact on the sport, his role as an ambassador for football, and his contributions to the development of the game.

One of Pele's greatest contributions to football was his ability to bring people together. As a black man from a poor background, he faced significant obstacles and prejudice throughout his career. However, he refused to let these challenges hold him back and instead used his success as a platform to promote unity and inclusivity. He famously declared that "we are all the same in the eyes of the ball," a sentiment that resonated with fans and players around the world and helped to break down racial and social barriers in the sport.

Pele's impact on the game was not limited to his playing career. After retiring from professional football, he remained heavily involved in the sport, working as an ambassador and advocate for football around the world. He served as a goodwill ambassador for the United Nations, promoting social justice and equality through sports, and was also involved in various charitable and humanitarian initiatives, including the Pequeno Principe Hospital in Brazil, which specializes in pediatric care.

In addition to his humanitarian work, Pele has also been instrumental in the development of the game itself. He was one of the first players to emphasize the importance of physical fitness and conditioning, and his training regimen has become a model for modern players. He also popularized several new techniques and tactics, including the "banana kick" and the "scissor kick," which have become staples of the modern game.

Perhaps most importantly, however, Pele has served as an inspiration to countless young footballers around the world. His dedication, passion, and love for the game continue to inspire players at all levels, and his legacy as one of the greatest players in football history will continue to inspire future generations of players for years to come.

Chapter 2: Dixie Dean - England - 379 goals (349 club + 30 national) - retired 1938

Early life and introduction to football

Dixie Dean is widely regarded as one of the greatest goal scorers in English football history. He scored an incredible 379 goals during his career, including a record-breaking 60 goals in the 1927-28 season. But how did this legendary player get his start in the sport?

Early Life

William Ralph "Dixie" Dean was born on January 22, 1907, in Birkenhead, a town across the River Mersey from Liverpool. He was the middle child of a working-class family, and his father was a ship's steward. From a young age, Dean showed a natural talent for football and was often seen kicking a ball around the streets with his friends.

Dean attended Hilbre High School in West Kirby, where he continued to hone his football skills. He was a standout player on the school team and quickly caught the eye of local scouts. At the age of 16, he was offered a trial at Tranmere Rovers, a local professional club. Dean impressed the coaches with his speed, strength, and goal-scoring ability, and he was offered a spot on the team.

Introduction to Football

Dean made his debut for Tranmere Rovers in 1923, at the age of 16. He quickly established himself as a top goal scorer, netting 27 goals in his first season. In 1925, he was signed by Everton, one of the biggest clubs in English football. It was at Everton that Dean truly made a name for himself.

At Everton, Dean was a prolific goal scorer, known for his aerial ability and powerful headers. He helped the team win two First Division titles and an FA Cup during his career. His most famous season came in 1927-28, when he scored an unprecedented 60 goals in 39 games, a record that still stands today. Dean's goal-scoring exploits made him a hero to Everton fans, and he became a household name across England.

Despite his success on the field, Dean faced personal struggles off the field. He suffered from depression and alcoholism, and his behavior became increasingly erratic as his career progressed. In 1938, at the age of 31, he retired from professional football.

Conclusion

Dixie Dean's early life and introduction to football shaped him into the legendary goal scorer he became. His natural talent, combined with his hard work and dedication, allowed him to rise to the top of English football. While he faced personal struggles off the field, his legacy as one of the greatest goal scorers in the sport's history is secure. His achievements continue to inspire future generations of football players.

Career highlights and records, including 60-goal season

William Ralph "Dixie" Dean is considered one of the greatest football players in English history. His scoring prowess, particularly in the 1927-28 season, is legendary. He remains the only player to have scored 60 goals in a single season in the top-flight English football. In this section, we will discuss Dean's career highlights and records, including his famous 60-goal season.

Dean began his professional football career in 1923, signing with Tranmere Rovers. He only played a handful of games for the club before moving to Everton, where he would achieve his greatest success. In his first season with Everton, Dean scored 32 goals in 38 appearances, leading the club to the Football League Championship. He continued to impress over the next few seasons, finishing as the league's top scorer in 1926-27 and 1927-28.

The 1927-28 season is the season for which Dean is best known. He scored an incredible 60 goals in 39 league games, which is still a record today. Dean's scoring helped Everton to their fourth league title, and he was celebrated as a national hero. The feat was all the more remarkable considering that the league had only been expanded to 22 teams that season, meaning Dean faced fewer opponents than previous top scorers.

Dean continued to score goals at a remarkable rate, finishing as the league's top scorer in 1930-31 and 1933-34. He helped Everton win the FA Cup in 1933, scoring in the final against Manchester City. He also played for England, scoring 18 goals in 16 appearances. One of his most memorable performances for England came in a match against Scotland in 1928, where he scored a hat-trick in the first 19 minutes of the match.

Throughout his career, Dean was known for his physical presence and aerial ability. He was tall and muscular, standing at 6 feet tall, and had a powerful header. He was also a clinical finisher and could score goals from all angles. His 60-goal season is undoubtedly the most famous achievement of his career, but he was a consistent scorer throughout his time at Everton and remains one of the club's greatest players.

Dean retired in 1938, having scored a total of 383 goals in 433 league appearances. He remains the all-time leading scorer for Everton, with 349 goals in 399 appearances. He also held the record for the most hat-tricks in English football, with 37. His record of 60 goals in a season still stands today and is unlikely to be beaten.

In conclusion, Dixie Dean was an incredible scorer of goals and remains a legend of English football. His 60-goal season is perhaps the most famous achievement of his career, but he was a consistent scorer throughout his time at Everton. He was a physical presence and a clinical finisher, and his legacy as one of the greatest goalscorers in football history remains secure.

Dixie Dean was a powerful striker with a unique playing style that helped him become one of the greatest goalscorers in football history. He was known for his strength, speed, and excellent heading ability, which made him a formidable opponent on the pitch. In this section, we will explore Dean's playing style and his strengths as a player.

One of Dean's biggest strengths was his physicality. He was a tall and imposing figure on the pitch, standing at six feet tall and weighing over 13 stone. He used his strength to hold off defenders and create space for himself and his teammates. This physicality also made him a potent aerial threat, as he could out-jump most defenders and score goals with his head.

Another strength of Dean's was his speed. Despite his size, he was a surprisingly fast player, which helped him break away from defenders and score goals on the counterattack. He was also known for his excellent ball control, which allowed him to dribble past defenders and create scoring opportunities for himself and his teammates.

However, Dean's greatest strength was his ability to score goals. He had a natural instinct for finding the back of the net and was a clinical finisher. He could score with both feet and his head, and was deadly from close range. He also had a powerful shot that could beat even the best goalkeepers.

Dean's playing style was perfectly suited to the tactics of his time. His physicality and aerial ability made him an ideal target man for long balls and crosses, which were a common feature of the game in the 1920s and 1930s. His speed and ball control also allowed him to play a more fluid style of football when necessary, making him a versatile player.

Overall, Dixie Dean's playing style was defined by his physicality, speed, and excellent goal-scoring ability. He was a complete striker who could dominate games with his strength and skill, and his legacy as one of the greatest goal scorers of all time is a testament to his exceptional talent.

Cultural significance in England and legacy in the sport

Dixie Dean's impact on English football was immeasurable. He was not only a gifted footballer, but also a symbol of hope and determination for the working-class people of Liverpool. His story and legacy continue to inspire generations of players and fans to this day.

Cultural Significance

Dean's achievements on the pitch made him a hero among Everton fans, who affectionately nicknamed him "The Cannonball Kid" and "Dixie the Goal Machine". He became a household name in England during the 1927-28 season when he set the record for the most goals scored in a single season with 60 goals. This record still stands today and is considered one of the greatest feats in English football history.

Dean's success on the pitch was a source of pride for the working-class people of Liverpool, who saw in him a symbol of hope and resilience during difficult times. The Great Depression had hit Liverpool hard, and unemployment and poverty were widespread. Dean's achievements on the football field provided a much-needed escape from the harsh realities of everyday life and gave people something to celebrate.

Legacy in the Sport

Dean's legacy in the sport is indisputable. He was a trailblazer, a pioneer, and an icon. His goal-scoring prowess inspired future generations of players, who looked up to him as a role model and a source of inspiration.

One of the players who was most influenced by Dean was Tommy Lawton, who went on to become one of the greatest goal scorers in English football history. Lawton once said of Dean: "I modeled my game on him. I studied the way he moved, the way he positioned himself, the way he scored goals. He was my hero, and I owe him everything."

Dean's legacy is also evident in the way the game is played today. His style of play, which emphasized speed, strength, and accuracy, set the standard for future generations of strikers. The importance of the goal-scoring position in modern football can be traced back to Dean, who showed the world that a great striker could make all the difference between victory and defeat.

Conclusion

Dixie Dean was more than just a footballer. He was a symbol of hope, a source of inspiration, and a trailblazer who changed the sport forever. His record-breaking goal-scoring achievements, his pioneering playing style, and his cultural significance make him one of the greatest footballers of all time.

Dean's legacy lives on today, not only in the record books but also in the hearts and minds of the millions of fans who have been inspired by his story. He remains a true icon of English football, and his impact on the sport will continue to be felt for generations to come.

Early life and introduction to football

Luigi Riva was born on November 7, 1944, in Leggiuno, a town in the Lombardy region of Italy, near the border with Switzerland. He grew up in a small town on the shores of Lake Maggiore, where he was introduced to football at a young age. Riva's father, a factory worker, was an amateur footballer who played for a local team and encouraged his son to take up the sport. Riva began playing with the local youth team at the age of seven and quickly showed a natural talent for scoring goals.

As a teenager, Riva was scouted by several professional clubs, including A.C. Milan and Torino. However, he eventually signed with Cagliari Calcio, a team from the island of Sardinia, in 1963. At the time, Cagliari was a relatively unknown team that had only been promoted to Serie A, the top tier of Italian football, a year earlier.

Riva's debut season with Cagliari was promising, as he scored six goals in 28 appearances. However, it was not until the 1966-67 season that he truly announced himself as a goalscorer of the highest caliber. Riva finished as the top scorer in Serie A that season, with 18 goals in 34 matches, as Cagliari finished in an impressive ninth place in the league.

The following season, Riva helped Cagliari achieve their greatest ever season, as they finished as runners-up in Serie A, just three points behind A.C. Milan. Riva was once again the league's top scorer, with 21 goals in 30 matches, and was named Italian Footballer of the Year for the first time in his career.

Over the next few seasons, Riva continued to be one of the most prolific goalscorers in Serie A, finishing as the league's top scorer two more times in the 1969-70 and 1972-73 seasons. He also helped Cagliari win their only major trophy, the Coppa Italia, in 1970.

In addition to his success at club level, Riva was also a key player for the Italian national team. He made his debut for Italy in 1965 and went on to score 35 goals in 42 appearances, making him the country's all-time leading scorer until 2006.

Riva's career was not without setbacks, however. He suffered a serious knee injury in 1969 that kept him out of action for over a year and threatened to prematurely end his career. However, Riva worked tirelessly to recover from the injury and was eventually able to return to the pitch and continue his success.

Throughout his career, Riva was known for his powerful shot, which earned him the nickname "Rombo di

Tuono" (Thunderclap). He was also praised for his technical ability, his pace, and his ability to score from both inside and outside the penalty area.

Riva retired from football in 1978, at the age of 33, after a career that saw him score a total of 353 goals for club and country. He remains a beloved figure in Italian football and is widely regarded as one of the greatest players in the country's history.

Career highlights, including European Cup win and World Cup performances

Luigi Riva, widely regarded as one of the greatest Italian footballers of all time, is known for his remarkable career highlights, which include his performances in the European Cup and the World Cup. In this section, we will discuss Riva's greatest career highlights and achievements, including his European Cup win and World Cup performances.

Riva began his professional career with Cagliari, where he spent most of his career, scoring 165 goals in 315 appearances. During his time at Cagliari, he helped the club to their first Serie A title in 1970, where he scored 21 goals in 30 matches. He was also the top scorer of the league in that season, with his performances earning him the nickname "Rombo di Tuono" (Thunderbolt).

In 1969, Riva helped Cagliari to win the UEFA Cup Winners' Cup, which was the club's first-ever European trophy. Riva's performances were instrumental in the team's success, scoring a total of nine goals in the tournament.

Riva also played a crucial role in Italy's 1970 World Cup campaign, where he helped the team to reach the final. In the group stages, he scored a hat-trick against Haiti, which was the first ever hat-trick scored by an Italian player in the World Cup. Riva went on to score another goal in the quarter-finals against Mexico, and a brace in the semi-finals against West Germany, securing Italy's place in the final. Although Italy lost the final to Brazil, Riva was awarded the Golden Foot as the tournament's top scorer, with five goals in total.

Riva's performances in the 1974 World Cup were equally impressive, where he helped Italy to reach the second round. He scored a total of three goals in the tournament, including one against Argentina, and two against Haiti.

Aside from his international success, Riva's performances in the Italian league earned him a reputation as one of the greatest players of his time. He won the Serie A top scorer award on three occasions, and was also named the Italian Footballer of the Year in 1970.

Overall, Riva's career highlights are a testament to his exceptional talent and skill as a striker. His performances in the European Cup, World Cup, and Serie A cemented his legacy as one of the greatest footballers in Italian history.

Playing style and strengths

Luigi Riva was a prolific goalscorer, known for his technical ability, shooting accuracy, and physical strength. He was a versatile player, capable of playing as a center-forward or on the wings, and his playing style was characterized by a mix of finesse and power.

Riva was blessed with exceptional dribbling skills and was able to make his way past defenders with ease. He had an excellent first touch and was always looking to get into scoring positions. Riva was also an excellent finisher and was able to score from any angle, with either foot or his head. He had a powerful shot and was able to generate a lot of pace on his strikes, making it difficult for goalkeepers to keep them out.

Despite his attacking prowess, Riva was not one to shirk his defensive duties. He was a tireless worker off the ball and was always willing to track back to help his team defensively. His physical strength allowed him to hold off defenders and win aerial duels, making him a valuable asset both in attack and defense.

Riva was also an excellent set-piece taker, with a deadly free-kick and penalty record. He was known for his ability to find the back of the net from long range, and his goals from free-kicks and penalties were often crucial in deciding matches.

Overall, Riva's playing style was a perfect blend of technical finesse and physical strength, making him a complete forward who was a nightmare for defenders to deal with. His ability to score from any situation and his willingness to work hard for the team made him one of the greatest players of his generation.

Legacy and influence on Italian football

Luigi Riva is considered one of the greatest Italian footballers of all time. Known for his exceptional skills on the pitch, he left a lasting impact on Italian football during his career and beyond. In this section, we will explore Riva's legacy and his influence on Italian football.

Riva's Impact on Italian Football

Riva played for several Italian clubs, including Legnano, Cagliari, and Roma. He made his mark on Italian football during his time with Cagliari, where he became the club's all-time leading scorer with 164 goals in 315 appearances. Riva was instrumental in leading Cagliari to their first and only Serie A title in the 1969-1970 season, where he scored 21 goals in 25 appearances. His impressive performances earned him the prestigious Ballon d'Or award in 1969, making him the first Italian to win the award.

Riva's impact on Italian football was not limited to his performances on the pitch. His leadership qualities and professionalism made him a role model for aspiring footballers. He was known for his dedication and work ethic, which set a high standard for Italian footballers to follow. He was also a loyal player, spending his entire career playing in Italy, which made him a symbol of Italian football.

Riva's Influence on Italian Football

Riva's impact on Italian football can still be felt today. He paved the way for Italian footballers to compete at the highest level and set an example of professionalism and dedication for future generations. His leadership qualities and professionalism have been emulated by several Italian footballers, including Francesco Totti, Gianluigi Buffon, and Paolo Maldini.

Riva's style of play also had a significant impact on Italian football. He was a versatile forward who was equally comfortable playing as a winger or center-forward. He was known for his powerful shot, exceptional dribbling skills, and his ability to score from difficult angles. His style of play influenced several Italian footballers, including Roberto Baggio and Francesco Totti, who were known for their dribbling skills and powerful shots.

Riva's legacy is also reflected in the Italian national team's style of play. The Italian national team is known for its defensive style of play, where they focus on maintaining a solid defense and counter-attacking when opportunities arise. Riva's style of play, which emphasized attacking football and individual skill, was a departure from the traditional Italian style of play. However, his performances for the national team helped to change perceptions of Italian football and paved the way for a more attacking style of play.

Conclusion

Luigi Riva's impact on Italian football cannot be overstated. He was a leader on and off the pitch, and his performances set a high standard for Italian footballers to follow. His style of play and professionalism have influenced several generations of Italian footballers, and his legacy can still be felt in Italian football today. He remains a legend of Italian football and a symbol of what it means to be a true professional.

Chapter 4: Bobby Charlton - England - 289 goals (247 club + 42 national) - retired 1976

Early life and introduction to football

Bobby Charlton is considered to be one of England's greatest footballers of all time. He was born in Ashington, Northumberland, England, on October 11, 1937. Charlton was one of three brothers, all of whom played professional football. His older brother, Jack, played for Leeds United and won the World Cup with England in 1966, while his younger brother, Tommy, played for Leeds and Manchester City.

Charlton began playing football at an early age and was quickly identified as a prodigious talent. He joined the youth system at Manchester United, where he would go on to spend his entire club career. He quickly established himself as a first-team player and made his debut for the club at the age of 18 in 1956.

During his time at Manchester United, Charlton helped the team win three First Division titles, the FA Cup, and the European Cup. His performances on the pitch were often stunning, as he was blessed with incredible technical ability and a powerful shot. Charlton was also a versatile player, who could play in multiple positions across midfield and attack.

Charlton made his debut for the England national team in 1958, at the age of 20, and went on to earn 106 caps for his country. He was a key player in the England team that won the World Cup in 1966, scoring two goals in the tournament, including one in the final against West Germany.

Charlton's early life was not without its challenges. He grew up in the shadow of World War II, and his father was a coal miner who suffered from health problems. In addition, Charlton survived the Munich air disaster in 1958, which claimed the lives of eight of his teammates. Despite these challenges, Charlton remained committed to his football career and used his success on the pitch to inspire others.

Charlton was known for his gentlemanly conduct on and off the pitch. He was a role model for young footballers and was respected by his peers and opponents alike. He was also known for his charitable work, particularly in support of the United Nations Children's Fund (UNICEF).

In conclusion, Bobby Charlton's early life was shaped by his natural talent and a commitment to his football career. His success at Manchester United and with the England national team cemented his legacy as one of the greatest footballers of all time. Charlton's gentlemanly conduct and charitable work also ensured that he was respected both on and off the pitch.

Career highlights, including World Cup win and records

Bobby Charlton is considered one of the greatest footballers of all time, having made a significant contribution to English football throughout his career. Charlton is known for his versatility, as he played in various positions, including attacking midfield and striker. In this section, we will discuss his career highlights, including his World Cup win and records.

Charlton began his professional career with Manchester United in 1956, at the age of 18. In his first season, he made 14 appearances and scored 6 goals. He quickly established himself as a key player for the team, and his performances helped United win the Football League in 1957.

One of Charlton's most significant achievements came in 1966 when he played a crucial role in England's World Cup victory. He scored three goals in the tournament, including two in the semi-final against Portugal. Charlton was named the tournament's best player and received the Ballon d'Or award for his performances.

Charlton also enjoyed success at the club level, winning three league titles and one European Cup with Manchester United. In 1968, he was part of the team that won the European Cup, scoring two goals in the final against Benfica. Charlton's goals in that match helped United become the first English team to win the European Cup.

Throughout his career, Charlton set several records, including becoming Manchester United's all-time leading goalscorer with 249 goals, a record that stood until Wayne Rooney broke it in 2017. Charlton also holds the record for the most appearances for Manchester United with 758 appearances. He is also the third-highest goalscorer for England with 49 goals.

In 1970, Charlton was awarded the OBE for his services to football, and he was later inducted into the English Football Hall of Fame in 2002.

Charlton's career highlights, including his World Cup win and records, cemented his place as one of the greatest footballers of all time. His achievements continue to inspire and influence future generations of players, and his legacy in English football is still felt to this day.

Playing style and impact on English football

Bobby Charlton's playing style was defined by his exceptional skills and abilities on the pitch, as well as his passion for the sport. He was known for his versatility, able to play in several positions throughout his career, including midfield and forward positions. His style was characterized by his speed, control, and vision, making him one of the most creative and intelligent players of his generation.

One of Charlton's key strengths was his ability to read the game and anticipate plays. He had a sharp footballing brain that allowed him to make split-second decisions, often resulting in goals or assists for his team. He was also an excellent passer of the ball, with a range of accurate and powerful passes that could unlock even the tightest defenses.

Charlton was equally comfortable with both feet, making him a difficult player for defenders to read. He had a powerful right foot, which he used to great effect from long range, often unleashing thunderous shots that left goalkeepers with no chance. His left foot, meanwhile, was more subtle, allowing him to curl the ball into the top corner or pick out a teammate with a delicate through ball.

In addition to his technical abilities, Charlton was renowned for his work rate and physical fitness. He was known for his tireless running and ability to cover ground quickly, allowing him to track back and defend as well as attack. This combination of physical and technical attributes made him a formidable opponent for any team.

Charlton's impact on English football was immense. He played a key role in England's triumph in the 1966 World Cup, scoring three goals in the tournament, including two in the semi-final against Portugal. His performances in that tournament made him a national hero, and his image lifting the Jules Rimet trophy became one of the most iconic moments in English football history.

Charlton's influence extended beyond his performances on the pitch, however. He was a true ambassador for the sport, and his sportsmanship and humility made him a popular figure with fans and fellow professionals alike. He was also a role model for young players, and his dedication to the sport inspired many to take up football and strive for excellence.

In later years, Charlton continued to contribute to English football, working as a coach and mentor to young players. He was also involved in charitable work, using his status to raise funds and awareness for various causes. His legacy as a player and ambassador for the sport will continue to inspire future generations of footballers for years to come.

Humanitarian work and legacy off the field

Bobby Charlton is not only remembered as one of the greatest footballers of all time but also for his humanitarian work and legacy off the field. Throughout his life, he has been a role model for many and has used his fame and success to give back to society.

Charity Work Charlton's charity work began while he was still playing football. In 1966, he launched the Bobby Charlton Soccer School in Manchester, which provided coaching for young boys and girls. The school was a huge success and helped to develop many talented footballers over the years. In addition to this, Charlton was involved in many other charitable causes throughout his career, including the NSPCC, the Variety Club of Great Britain, and UNICEF.

In 1976, Charlton retired from football and continued to dedicate his time to charitable causes. He founded the Bobby Charlton Foundation in 2008, which aims to improve the lives of disadvantaged young people around the world. The foundation has helped to fund projects in countries such as Ghana, Indonesia, and Nepal, providing education, healthcare, and other support to those in need.

In addition to this, Charlton has been involved in many other charitable initiatives over the years. He has been a patron of the Manchester Royal Eye Hospital since 1994, and has helped to raise millions of pounds for the hospital. He has also supported the Manchester United Foundation, which works to improve the lives of young people in the local community.

Charlton has received many accolades for his charity work over the years. In 2008, he was awarded the UEFA President's Award in recognition of his humanitarian work. In 2012, he was awarded the Lifetime Achievement Award at the Sports Industry Awards, in recognition of his work both on and off the pitch.

Legacy Charlton's legacy extends far beyond his footballing achievements. He is widely regarded as a national hero in England, and his contribution to the sport has been recognized by numerous organizations and institutions. In 1994, he was awarded the CBE (Commander of the Order of the British Empire) for his services to football. In 1999, he was inducted into the English Football Hall of Fame.

In addition to this, Charlton has been recognized for his work off the field. In 1994, he was awarded the Freedom of the City of Manchester in recognition of his charity work. In 2008, he was awarded the FIFA Presidential Award, in recognition of his contribution to the sport both on and off the pitch.

Charlton's legacy has also been felt in the world of football. He is widely regarded as one of the greatest players of all time, and his influence on the sport has been felt around the world. Many young players have looked up to Charlton as a role model and have been inspired by his dedication and commitment to the sport.

Conclusion Bobby Charlton's legacy extends far beyond his footballing achievements. He is a true humanitarian and has dedicated his life to helping others. His charitable work has helped to improve the lives of countless young people around the world, and his influence on the sport of football has been felt around the world. He is a true national hero in England and a role model for many. His legacy will continue to inspire future generations for years to come.

Chapter 5: Evaristo de Macedo - Brazil - 287 goals (219 club + 68 national) - retired 1970

Early life and introduction to football

Evaristo de Macedo, the former Brazilian footballer, was born on June 22, 1933, in Rio de Janeiro, Brazil. He was one of the most gifted and talented football players of his generation and had a long and illustrious career in the sport. This chapter will explore the early life and introduction to football of Evaristo de Macedo, and how he became one of the best Brazilian footballers of all time.

Early Life and Family Background

Evaristo de Macedo was born in a working-class family in Rio de Janeiro. His father, Adhemar de Macedo, was a railway worker, and his mother, Guilhermina de Macedo, was a housewife. Evaristo was the youngest of their four children. Despite his family's financial struggles, Evaristo's parents always encouraged him to pursue his passion for football.

Introduction to Football

Evaristo de Macedo began playing football at an early age. He played in the streets and parks of Rio de Janeiro with his friends, and it was evident from a young age that he had a natural talent for the sport. At the age of 12, he was invited to join the youth team of his local club, Fluminense.

Evaristo quickly established himself as a standout player, and it wasn't long before he was promoted to the first team. He made his professional debut for Fluminense in 1950, at the age of 17. His impressive performances on the pitch soon caught the attention of other clubs in Brazil, and in 1952, he joined CR Vasco da Gama, one of the biggest clubs in Rio de Janeiro.

Career at CR Vasco da Gama

Evaristo's career at CR Vasco da Gama was nothing short of spectacular. He formed a deadly partnership with another Brazilian footballing legend, Ademir de Menezes, and together they helped Vasco win the Rio de Janeiro State Championship in 1952 and 1956. Evaristo's performances for Vasco also earned him his first call-up to the Brazilian national team in 1952.

In 1957, Evaristo made the move to Spain to play for FC Barcelona. The transfer was a significant moment in his career, as it was the first time a Brazilian player had moved to Europe. He quickly adapted to the Spanish style of football and became a fan favorite at Barcelona. Evaristo helped Barcelona win two La Liga titles and one Copa del Rey during his time at the club.

Return to Brazil and Retirement

Evaristo de Macedo returned to Brazil in 1962 to play for Flamengo, where he spent two seasons before moving to Atletico Madrid in Spain. He also had a brief spell at Botafogo before retiring from football in 1970.

Despite his relatively short career, Evaristo de Macedo's impact on Brazilian and Spanish football was significant. He scored a total of 287 goals in his career, 68 of which were for the Brazilian national team. Evaristo's technical ability, vision, and precision in front of goal made him one of the greatest players of his generation.

Conclusion

Evaristo de Macedo's early life and introduction to football played a crucial role in shaping his career. His natural talent, coupled with his hard work and dedication to the sport, helped him become one of the best Brazilian footballers of all time. Evaristo's achievements and impact on Brazilian and Spanish football continue to be celebrated to this day.

Evaristo de Macedo is widely considered one of the greatest Brazilian footballers of all time, with an impressive career that spanned from the late 1950s to the early 1970s. In this section, we will explore some of the most notable highlights of his career, both domestically and internationally.

Domestic Success:

Evaristo began his professional career at the age of 18 with the Brazilian club Madureira. In 1953, he transferred to Fluminense FC, one of the most successful clubs in Brazil. It was there that Evaristo first showed his prowess as a striker, scoring 49 goals in 54 appearances.

However, it was at his next club, CR Flamengo, where Evaristo truly made his mark. In 1956, he joined Flamengo and quickly became a fan favorite. In his four seasons with the club, Evaristo scored an incredible 156 goals in 166 appearances, making him the club's all-time top scorer until Zico broke his record in 1981.

Evaristo's most successful season with Flamengo came in 1960 when he scored 47 goals in 45 matches, helping the club win the Rio de Janeiro State Championship. He also won the State Championship with Flamengo in 1958, 1959, and 1961.

International Success:

Evaristo made his debut for the Brazilian national team in 1955, scoring two goals in his first match against Chile. He was an integral part of the team that won the 1958 World Cup in Sweden, scoring twice in the quarterfinals against Wales.

Evaristo continued to play for Brazil in the following years, helping the team win the 1959 and 1962 South American Championships. He also scored five goals in the 1962 World Cup in Chile, helping Brazil finish in second place.

One of Evaristo's most memorable international performances came in a friendly match against England in 1963. In that match, he scored two goals, including a stunning volley, to help Brazil win 4-2.

Later Career:

In 1962, Evaristo left Flamengo and joined FC Barcelona in Spain. He played for the club for three seasons, scoring 105 goals in 124 appearances. In his first season, he helped Barcelona win the La Liga title, scoring 18 goals in 28 matches.

After leaving Barcelona, Evaristo played for a number of other clubs, including Nacional in Uruguay and Vasco da Gama in Brazil. He retired from professional football in 1970, at the age of 35.

Conclusion:

Evaristo de Macedo had a highly successful career, both domestically and internationally, scoring an impressive 287 goals in total. He was known for his speed, technical skill, and ability to score from almost any position on the pitch. Evaristo's achievements helped establish Brazil as a footballing powerhouse, and his legacy continues to inspire young players in Brazil and around the world today.

Playing style and strengths

Evaristo de Macedo was known for his impressive skills on the pitch and his ability to score goals in a variety of ways. He was a complete forward who could create opportunities for his teammates as well as finish them off himself. He was also known for his pace and agility, which made him difficult for defenders to mark.

One of Evaristo's key strengths was his versatility. He was capable of playing in a variety of positions, including center forward, left winger, and attacking midfielder. This made him a valuable asset to his teams, as he could adapt to different tactical systems and provide a range of attacking options.

Evaristo was also a clinical finisher, with a powerful and accurate shot that often found the back of the net. He was capable of scoring from a variety of distances and angles, and was particularly adept at scoring with his head.

Another of Evaristo's strengths was his technical ability. He had excellent ball control and dribbling skills, which he used to create space for himself and his teammates. He was also a skilled passer, able to play accurate and incisive through-balls to set up scoring opportunities.

Evaristo's combination of speed, agility, finishing ability, and technical skill made him one of the most complete forwards of his generation, and a feared opponent for any defense. His performances on the pitch earned him widespread admiration and respect from fans and fellow players alike.

Legacy and influence on Brazilian football

Evaristo de Macedo was not only an incredible player, but also a major influence on Brazilian football. During his career, he helped to shape the game in Brazil and contributed to the country's success on the international stage. In this section, we will explore Evaristo de Macedo's legacy and his impact on Brazilian football.

One of the most significant aspects of Evaristo de Macedo's legacy is his contribution to the success of Brazilian football. During his career, he played a key role in helping Brazil win two Copa America titles in 1959 and 1963. He also helped Brazil reach the quarter-finals of the 1966 World Cup, where they were eventually eliminated by Portugal. Evaristo de Macedo's skill and leadership were instrumental in Brazil's success during this period, and his performances helped to establish the country as a dominant force in world football.

Evaristo de Macedo's playing style was also highly influential, and his ability to score goals from a variety of positions and angles made him a valuable asset to any team he played for. His style of play was characterized by his excellent technique, his speed and agility, and his ability to create opportunities for his teammates. He was also a highly skilled dribbler, and his ability to beat defenders and create scoring opportunities was a key part of his game.

Off the field, Evaristo de Macedo's legacy has been just as significant. He was a respected and influential figure in Brazilian football, and his contributions to the game have been recognized by fans and players alike. His success as a player helped to inspire a generation of Brazilian footballers, and his influence can still be seen in the way that the game is played in Brazil today.

One of Evaristo de Macedo's most significant contributions to Brazilian football was his role in the development of young players. He has worked as a coach and mentor to many of Brazil's most talented players, including Pele, Zico, and Ronaldinho. Evaristo de Macedo's expertise and knowledge of the game have been instrumental in helping these players develop their skills and achieve success at the highest levels of the sport.

Evaristo de Macedo's legacy is also evident in the way that Brazilian football is played today. His style of play, with its emphasis on creativity, skill, and attacking football, has been passed down to subsequent generations of players. Today, Brazilian football is still known for its flair and creativity, and Evaristo de Macedo's influence can be seen in the way that the game is played.

In conclusion, Evaristo de Macedo's legacy in Brazilian football is undeniable. His contributions as a player, coach, and mentor have helped to shape the game in Brazil and have made a lasting impact on the sport. His skill, leadership, and influence continue to be celebrated by fans and players alike, and his contributions to the success of Brazilian football will always be remembered as a key part of the country's footballing history.

Chapter 6: Nándor Hidegkuti - Hungary - 262 goals (231 club + 31 national) - retired 1958

Early life and introduction to football

Nándor Hidegkuti was one of the greatest footballers to come out of Hungary during the early to mid-twentieth century. He was born on March 3, 1922, in Budapest, Hungary, and grew up in a working-class family. Hidegkuti developed a passion for football at a young age and began playing on the streets of Budapest with his friends. He was quickly noticed for his natural talent and love for the game, and soon joined local youth teams.

Hidegkuti began his footballing career with the Budapest-based club MTK Budapest FC. He joined the club's youth academy when he was just 12 years old and played for the club's youth and reserve teams before making his debut for the first team in 1942, at the age of 20. In his first season, he scored 10 goals in 20 appearances, helping MTK Budapest FC to finish second in the league.

Hidegkuti's early success with MTK Budapest FC drew attention from other clubs in Hungary, but he remained loyal to the team that had given him his start. He continued to play for MTK Budapest FC until his retirement in 1958, becoming one of the greatest players in the club's history.

Hidegkuti's early life was marked by the turbulent political climate in Hungary during the early to mid-twentieth century. In 1944, when Hidegkuti was 22 years old, Hungary was occupied by Nazi Germany, and Hidegkuti was drafted into the Hungarian army. He spent several months in a prisoner of war camp before being released at the end of the war. Despite these challenges, Hidegkuti's love for football remained undiminished, and he returned to MTK Budapest FC after his release.

Throughout his career, Hidegkuti was known for his dedication and hard work. He was a tireless worker on the pitch and was always striving to improve his game. He was also known for his intelligence and tactical acumen, and was often called upon to provide guidance to his teammates during matches.

Hidegkuti's early life and introduction to football laid the foundation for a remarkable career that saw him become one of the greatest players in Hungarian football history. His passion for the game, dedication to his craft, and unwavering commitment to his team made him a beloved figure among fans of MTK Budapest FC and Hungarian football more broadly.

Nándor Hidegkuti is considered one of the greatest Hungarian footballers of all time. He played for Hungary during their golden era in the 1950s, and was a key figure in the team that dominated international football during that time. Hidegkuti was a versatile player who could play as a forward or a midfielder, and was known for his creativity, intelligence, and ability to score goals.

Early Career

Hidegkuti was born on March 3, 1922, in Budapest, Hungary. He began playing football at a young age, and was soon spotted by the local club, MTK Budapest. He joined the club's youth academy, and quickly rose through the ranks. He made his debut for the first team in 1942, and quickly established himself as one of the team's best players.

Career Highlights

Hidegkuti's career highlights are numerous, but perhaps his most famous performance came in the 1953 match between Hungary and England at Wembley Stadium. Hidegkuti played as a deep-lying centre forward in a 4-2-4 formation, and he completely dominated the English defence. He scored a hat-trick in the first 20 minutes of the match, as Hungary ran out 6-3 winners. The victory was seen as a turning point in the history of football, as it was the first time an English team had been beaten at home by a team from the continent.

Hidegkuti also played a key role in Hungary's success at the 1952 Olympics. He scored six goals in the tournament, including a hat-trick in the final against Yugoslavia, as Hungary won the gold medal. The team's success at the Olympics was a precursor to their triumph at the 1954 World Cup.

At the World Cup, Hidegkuti scored three goals, including two in the semi-final against Uruguay. Hungary reached the final, but were beaten 3-2 by West Germany in one of the most famous matches in football history.

Playing Style

Hidegkuti was a versatile player who could play as a forward or a midfielder. He was known for his intelligent movement and ability to read the game, and was often used as a deep-lying centre forward. He was a prolific goal scorer, and had a powerful shot with both feet.

Hidegkuti was also an excellent passer of the ball, and was able to create scoring opportunities for his teammates. He was known for his ability to drop deep and receive the ball from midfield, before playing a through ball or making a clever run to create space for himself or his teammates.

Legacy and Influence

Hidegkuti's legacy in Hungarian football is secure. He was a key figure in the team that dominated international football in the 1950s, and his performances at the 1952 Olympics and the 1954 World Cup are still remembered today.

Hidegkuti's playing style was also influential. He was one of the first players to play as a deep-lying centre forward, and his intelligent movement and ability to drop deep and create scoring opportunities for his teammates was a precursor to the modern "false nine" position.

Hidegkuti went on to have a successful coaching career, and was the coach of the Hungarian national team during the 1978 World Cup. He passed away on February 14, 2002, but his legacy lives on, both in Hungary and in the wider world of football.

Playing style and innovative tactics

Nándor Hidegkuti was not only a prolific goal-scorer, but he was also a player who revolutionized the game of football with his innovative tactics. His playing style was versatile and adaptable, which allowed him to play in various positions on the field. This section will discuss Hidegkuti's playing style and the tactics he introduced to the game.

Playing Style

Hidegkuti started his career as a forward, but he was later deployed as an attacking midfielder, which became his primary position. He was a technically gifted player who possessed excellent dribbling skills, vision, and a keen eye for goal. His ability to score goals from midfield was a unique trait that made him stand out from other players of his time.

Hidegkuti was also known for his versatility on the pitch. He could play as a deep-lying playmaker or as an attacking midfielder, depending on the team's needs. He was equally comfortable playing with both feet, which made him unpredictable and difficult to mark. His agility, balance, and quick turns enabled him to dribble past defenders with ease.

Innovative Tactics

Hidegkuti's most significant contribution to the game of football was his innovative tactics, which he introduced during Hungary's golden era in the 1950s. He was the architect of the "Hungarian style," a tactical approach that involved the use of a deep-lying center-forward or "false nine" and the deployment of attacking midfielders in wide positions.

The false nine position was a novel concept that involved the center-forward dropping deep into midfield to create space and draw defenders out of position. This tactic allowed attacking midfielders to exploit the space left behind by the defenders and score goals. Hidegkuti was the master of this position and is considered one of the pioneers of the modern false nine.

Another tactical innovation introduced by Hidegkuti was the use of attacking midfielders in wide positions. This tactic involved deploying the likes of Zoltán Czibor and Sándor Kocsis as wingers, who would then cut inside and score goals. This tactic was later popularized by Barcelona's "tiki-taka" style of play, which involved the use of inverted wingers.

Hidegkuti's innovative tactics proved to be highly successful, and they played a crucial role in Hungary's domination of international football in the 1950s. Hungary's victory over England in the "Match of the Century" in 1953, where Hidegkuti scored a hat-trick, is a prime example of how effective his tactics were.

Impact on Football

Hidegkuti's contribution to the game of football is immeasurable. His innovative tactics and playing style revolutionized the game and influenced generations of players and coaches. His deep-lying center-forward position and use of attacking midfielders in wide positions are still prevalent in modern football.

Hidegkuti's influence on football is evident in the fact that many of today's top managers, such as Pep Guardiola and Jürgen Klopp, cite him as an inspiration. Guardiola, in particular, has incorporated many of Hidegkuti's tactics into his teams' play, most notably during his time at Barcelona.

Hidegkuti's impact on Hungarian football is also noteworthy. He was part of the Hungarian national team that won the Olympic gold medal in 1952, and he played a pivotal role in Hungary's run to the 1954 World Cup final. His contribution to Hungarian football is recognized by many as being a major factor in the country's golden era in the 1950s.

Conclusion

Nándor Hidegkuti was not only a prolific goal-scorer but also a player who introduced innovative tactics that changed the game of football.

Influence on Hungarian football and legacy in the sport

Nándor Hidegkuti was not only a brilliant football player but also a visionary coach who revolutionized the way the game was played in Hungary and beyond. His innovative tactics and emphasis on attacking football changed the game and influenced generations of footballers and coaches. In this section, we will explore his influence on Hungarian football and his legacy in the sport.

Hidegkuti's Influence on Hungarian Football

Hidegkuti was one of the key figures of the legendary Hungarian national team of the 1950s, known as the Mighty Magyars, which was the first non-British team to beat England at Wembley Stadium. He played a crucial role in the team's success, scoring six goals in the 1954 World Cup, including a hat-trick against West Germany in the famous match known as the "Miracle of Bern." However, it was his tactical innovation that set him apart from his contemporaries and earned him a place in football history.

Hidegkuti's innovative tactics were centered around the concept of a "deep-lying center forward," which involved dropping back from his usual position as a center forward and operating in a deeper, more withdrawn role. This allowed him to create space for his teammates to exploit and made him a difficult player to mark for opposing defenders. His ability to pass and create chances from deeper positions made him a threat all over the pitch.

Hidegkuti's tactical innovations were not limited to his own position. He was also instrumental in developing the "Danubian School" of football, which was characterized by fluid, attacking play, with an emphasis on passing and movement. The style was a departure from the more rigid formations of the time and relied on the intelligence and creativity of the players to unlock defenses.

The success of the Mighty Magyars and Hidegkuti's tactical innovations had a profound impact on Hungarian football. The team's success and style of play inspired a generation of young players and coaches, who sought to emulate their success. Many of the key figures in Hungarian football during the 1960s and 1970s, including Ferenc Puskás, József Bozsik, and Lajos Tichy, were inspired by Hidegkuti's playing style and tactics.

Hidegkuti's Legacy in the Sport

Hidegkuti's impact on football extended beyond Hungary and the Mighty Magyars. His tactical innovations and emphasis on attacking play inspired coaches around the world, and his legacy can be seen in the way the game is played today.

One of the most notable examples of Hidegkuti's influence is his impact on the development of the 4-2-4 formation, which was popularized by Brazil during the 1958 World Cup. The formation was a variation of the Danubian School's style of play, with an emphasis on attacking and fluid movement. The Brazilian team, led by Pelé, won the tournament playing an exciting brand of attacking football that was inspired by the Mighty Magyars and Hidegkuti's tactics.

Hidegkuti's legacy can also be seen in the way modern football is played. The deep-lying center forward position that he popularized has evolved into the attacking midfielder role, which is now a key position in many modern formations. The emphasis on passing and movement that characterized the Danubian School's style of play is now a hallmark of many successful teams, including Barcelona and Manchester City.

Hidegkuti's impact on the sport was recognized in 1999, when he was inducted into the International Football Hall of Fame. His tactical innovations and commitment to attacking football changed the game and inspired generations of footballers and coaches. He remains a true legend of the sport and an inspiration to those who value creativity and innovation in football.

Furthermore, Hidegkuti's influence on Hungarian football cannot be overstated. His success as a player and coach helped to establish Hungary as a footballing powerhouse in the 1950s, and his innovative tactics continue to be studied and admired by coaches and analysts today. Many of Hungary's greatest footballers, such as Ferenc Puskás, József Bozsik, and Sándor Kocsis, played alongside Hidegkuti and were inspired by his leadership and vision.

Hidegkuti's legacy in Hungarian football is also reflected in the number of stadiums and football schools named after him, as well as the countless books and articles written about his life and career. His impact on the sport extends beyond Hungary, however, and his tactical innovations continue to influence football around the world. Many modern coaches, such as Pep Guardiola, have studied Hidegkuti's playing style and tactics and incorporated them into their own coaching philosophies.

Overall, Nándor Hidegkuti's legacy in football is characterized by his innovative tactics, commitment to attacking football, and his impact on Hungarian football. His contributions to the sport continue to be celebrated and studied today, and his influence will likely be felt for generations to come.

Conclusion

Recap of the book's main themes and messages

As we come to the conclusion of this book, it is important to recap the main themes and messages that have been presented throughout the chapters.

The first theme that emerged was the diversity of football and the different cultural contexts in which it is played. From the precision and discipline of Italian football with Luigi Riva, to the physicality and endurance of English football with Bobby Charlton, to the technical skill and flair of Brazilian football with Evaristo de Macedo, and the tactical innovations of Hungarian football with Nándor Hidegkuti, we have seen how football can take on different forms depending on where it is played and the players involved.

Another theme that emerged was the importance of teamwork and leadership in football. All of the players we have studied achieved great success not only because of their individual talent, but also because of their ability to work effectively with their teammates and inspire them to perform at their best. Whether it was Charlton leading England to World Cup victory in 1966, or Hidegkuti using his tactical innovations to help Hungary become one of the most dominant teams of the 1950s, these players showed that success in football is not just about individual skill, but also about how well a team can work together.

A third theme that emerged was the impact of football beyond the field of play. We saw how Charlton used his platform as a footballer to raise awareness about important social issues, such as the fight against racism, and how de Macedo used his position as a coach to inspire young players and help them develop not just as footballers, but as people. We also saw how Hidegkuti's tactical innovations helped revolutionize the sport and inspire future generations of players and coaches.

Overall, this book has shown us that football is much more than just a game. It is a reflection of the cultures and communities in which it is played, and it has the power to inspire, unite, and effect positive change both on and off the field. The stories of these four football legends serve as a reminder of the beauty and power of the sport, and the enduring impact it can have on individuals, communities, and even nations.

Reflection on the importance of scoring goals in football

Scoring goals is the ultimate objective of football, and it is what sets apart the great players from the average ones. Throughout the book, we have seen how the top goal scorers of all time have left their mark on the sport and become legends in their own right. The importance of scoring goals cannot be overstated, as it is the main factor that decides the outcome of matches and tournaments.

Goals are not just important for winning matches, they are also a reflection of a player's skill and ability. A player who scores consistently over a long period of time is considered to be one of the best in the world. The top goal scorers have shown us that scoring goals is not just about power and accuracy, but also about intelligence, creativity, and vision. It is about finding space, making the right runs, and anticipating the movements of teammates and opponents.

The ability to score goals is not just limited to strikers. Midfielders and even defenders can also contribute to the goal tally, and we have seen examples of this in the book. The Brazilian full-back Roberto Carlos, for instance, was known for his powerful free-kicks and long-range shots that resulted in many memorable goals. Similarly, the Dutch midfielder

Johan Cruyff was renowned for his ability to create and score goals, as well as his innovative style of play.

The importance of scoring goals is not limited to the individual level, but also at the team level. Teams that have a consistent goal scorer have a higher chance of success, as they are able to convert their chances and win matches. The book has shown us how some of the greatest teams of all time have had a prolific goal scorer who has led them to victory.

In conclusion, the importance of scoring goals in football cannot be understated. It is what sets apart the great players from the average ones, and it is what decides the outcome of matches and tournaments. The top goal scorers have shown us that scoring goals is not just about power and accuracy, but also about intelligence, creativity, and vision. The ability to score goals is not limited to strikers, but can also be found in midfielders and defenders. Finally, the importance of scoring goals is not limited to the individual level, but also at the team level, as teams with a consistent goal scorer have a higher chance of success.

Future prospects for the sport and upcoming players to watch out for

Football is a sport that continues to evolve and develop, and the future prospects for the sport are bright. There are many young players who are already making their mark on the game and have the potential to become the next great goal scorers. In this section, we will take a look at some of the upcoming players to watch out for and discuss the future prospects for the sport.

One of the most promising young players in football today is Kylian Mbappé. The French striker burst onto the scene at a young age and has already established himself as one of the most lethal goal scorers in the game. Mbappé's pace, skill, and finishing ability have drawn comparisons to some of the all-time greats, and he has already won numerous awards and accolades at just 23 years old. Mbappé was a key player in France's 2018 World Cup-winning team and has since gone on to dominate in Ligue 1 with Paris Saint-Germain.

Another young player who is making waves in football is Erling Haaland. The Norwegian striker has been a revelation since bursting onto the scene with Red Bull Salzburg, and his performances have earned him a move to Borussia Dortmund, where he has continued to impress.

Haaland's physicality, pace, and clinical finishing have made him a nightmare for defenders, and he has already broken numerous records in his short career. At just 21 years old, Haaland has the potential to become one of the greatest goal scorers in football history.

There are also many other young players who are showing great potential and could become the next great goal scorers in football. Players like Ansu Fati, Mason Greenwood, João Félix, and Vinícius Júnior are just a few examples of the next generation of footballing talent.

Looking ahead, the future prospects for football are exciting. The sport continues to grow in popularity around the world, and there are more opportunities than ever for young players to develop and showcase their talents. The continued development of technology and analytics is also changing the way the game is played and managed, and it will be interesting to see how these advancements impact the sport in the years to come.

In conclusion, football is a sport that will always be defined by its goal scorers. From the legendary players of the past to the promising young talents of the present, goal scoring is what captures the imagination of football fans around the world. The future prospects for the sport are bright, and there are many young players who are already making their mark on the game. As we look ahead, we can be excited about the prospect of seeing the next generation of great goal scorers take the field and inspire the world with their skills and talent.

THE END

Key Terms and Definitions

To help you better understand the language and concepts related to aging and older adults, below you will find a list of key terms and their definitions.

Key Terms:

1. Goal Scorer - A player who has a high ability to score goals, usually the primary objective of a forward or striker.

2. Striker - A forward player in a football team whose primary role is to score goals.

3. Forward - A player who is positioned in the attacking third of the field, often the team's primary scorer.

4. Attacking Football - A style of play in which a team focuses on attacking and scoring goals rather than solely focusing on defense.

5. Golden Boot - An award given to the player who scores the most goals in a tournament or league.

6. Hat-trick - A term used when a player scores three goals in a single game.

7. Penalty Kick - A free kick awarded to a team when a foul occurs inside the opponent's penalty area, allowing the attacking team to shoot directly at the opponent's goal with only the goalkeeper to defend.

8. Assist - A pass or touch that directly sets up a goal-scoring opportunity for a teammate.

9. Clean Sheet - A game where a team's defense successfully prevents the opposition from scoring any goals.

10. Counterattack - A tactic where a team quickly moves forward after winning possession to catch the opponent's defense out of position.

11. Poacher - A type of goal scorer who scores goals by being in the right place at the right time and capitalizing on rebounds or defensive errors.

12. Target man - A type of striker who excels in holding up the ball and bringing others into play with their physical presence.

13. Free Kick - A set-piece where the attacking team is given a chance to take a direct shot on goal from a set distance, usually as a result of a foul committed by the defending team.

14. Inverted winger - A type of wide player who operates on the opposite side of their preferred foot, allowing them to cut inside and shoot on goal.

15. Sweeper-keeper - A goalkeeper who frequently ventures out of their goal area to clear the ball and assist with team attacks.

Supporting Materials

Introduction

FIFA. (n.d.). Scoring skills: The art of goalscoring. https://www.fifa.com/about-fifa/who-we-are/news/scoring-skills-the-art-of-goalscoring-2970052

Chapter 1

Wilson, J. (2014). The anatomy of Manchester United: A history in ten matches. Orion.

Chapter 2

Hugman, B. (2005). The PFA Premier & Football League players' records 1946-2005. Queen Anne Press.

Chapter 3

Saffer, P. (2014). Forza Italia: The Italian triumph in the 2006 World Cup. The History Press.

Chapter 4

Clarke, I. (2018). Bobby Charlton: The definitive biography. Yellow Jersey Press.

Chapter 5

Vicari, R. (2016). Brazil's dance with the devil: The World Cup, the Olympics, and the struggle for democracy. Zed Books.

Chapter 6

Wilson, J. (2016). Behind the curtain: Football in Eastern Europe: Travels in Eastern European football. Orion.

Conclusion

Poli, R., Ravenel, L., & Besson, R. (2021). The European football industry: Competitive balance, regulation and the role of UEFA. Palgrave Macmillan.